THE TWO RONNIES
But First — The News

A Star Original

The news, Ronnies style, has become the trademark of the most successful comedy team to appear on our screens. It provides the hilarious vehicle for Barker and Corbett to exercise their witty repartee with some of the most original jests presented on television over the past five years.

Compiled by Ronnies' scriptwriter Peter Vincent, this is the first in a series of sidesplitting selections that will bring tears to your eyes. Unless, of course, you too happen to be a victim of plastic surgeon Sir Hartley Horsefall, sued by one of his lady clients because of shoddy workmanship and high prices — the lady in question stated: 'I realised what a bad job Sir Hartley had done on me when a friend took me aside and said confidingly, "A word in your nose . . . You're paying through the ear for everything!" '

With gratitude to the correspondents who risked death and worse to gather these News Items from numerous corners of the globe. Oh, all right, they made them up . . .

Peter Bain, Alec Baron, John Bartlett, Norman Beedle, Robert Belford, Dennis Berson, Ray Binns, Alex Brown and Pat Murray, Mary Butcher, Stuart Campbell, Garry Chambers, Syd Clark, Mike Cole and John McGrouther, Graham Deykin, Dave Dutton, Pete Edwards, Stan Edwards, Wyn Edwards, Harry Evans, Ernest Forbes, Cathie Foote, Neville Gurnhill, Frank Hickman, Les Higgins, Howard Imber, Desmond Jones, Tudor Jones, Dorothy Kilmurry-Hall, Frank Kirkbride, John Lloyd, Roy Lomax, David McKellar, Tom Magee-Englefield, Malcolm Mather, Tony Mather, Fred Metcalf, Mike Meys, Philip Munnoch, Alex Myles and Les Lilley, Ralph Morris, David Nobbs, Wendy Norton, Gavin Osbon, Terry Ravenscroft, David Renwick, Tony Rich, Laurie Rowley, John Sayle, Robert Scott, Eric Searle, Charles Shiells, Robin Soans, Austin Steele, Gordon Stretch, Hugh Stuckey, Terry Treloar, Len Walker, David Webb, Gerald Wiley and Stan Wootton.

THE TWO RONNIES
But First - The News

Compiled by Peter Vincent

A STAR BOOK
published by
the Paperback Division of
W. H. ALLEN & Co. Ltd.

A Star Book
Published in 1977
by the Paperback Division of
W. H. Allen & Co. Ltd.
A Howard and Wyndham Company
44 Hill Street, London W1X 8LB
Reprinted 1977 (twice)

Printed in Great Britain by
Richard Clay (The Chaucer Press) Ltd,
Bungay, Suffolk

ISBN 0 352 39899 X

FOREWORD

It it almost as hard for me to start this piece -
the first of its kind that I've ever attempted -
as it would be for Ronnie and I to open the
show without these cherished News Items. I am
going to prepare myself for the task in the
manner of the true writer. I shall retire to my
study - a warm room facing the garden,
decorated and carpeted in guardsman's red (see
Brolac colour chart) with curtains in a bold
black and white houndstooth (see David Hicks'
Living with Style). I am looking out on Surrey
heathers and silver birches and *still* wondering
how to start. I have around me the
paraphernalia of the essayist, a cup of strong,
sweet, dark brown coffee (see West Wickham
Cash and Carry), a pack of half used Kleenex
(see Cole Porter's *Song Book),* a signed picture
of the Duke of Windsor (signed by my cousin,
Bert, that is), and a pack of vivid green
Japanese pentels jammed casually into a
Dartington glass tankard. For this one foreword
I have spent a fortune in Rymans - three packs
of paper in different sizes, all colours of pens,
paper clips, bulldog clips, drawing pins, two
diaries, a pocket filing system, three reels of
Sellotape, two boxes of refills for a pen I don't
possess and I am *still* wondering how to start.
I put my pen down, finish the coffee and then I
have the most marvellous idea. I'll ring Spike
Mullins and get him to do it.

RONNIE CORBETT 1977

FURTHER FOREWORD

These "news items", the pick of all those
Ronnie Corbett and I have delivered from
behind that double desk, have become such a
trade-mark of the show that I cannot imagine
starting and finishing in any other way.
Obviously, I remember with affection some of
the gags — the elephant doing a ton on the M1;
the contortionist who had come from Australia
to look up his relatives; and the stunt-man who
fell sixty feet, landing on Raquel Welch (his
condition was described later as extremely
comfortable), but for the most part they had
'flowed away down the dark stream of memory'
as Lionel Blair once put it. What a treat, then,
to sample them once again in this splendid and
rib-tickling selection. I hope you enjoy them as
much as I did.

RONNIE BARKER 1976

INDECENTLY FOREWORD

The audience are comfortably in their seats, the cameramen at their posts and there is five minutes to go before the start of another edition of *The Two Ronnies* series, yet Messrs. Corbett and Barker are still closetted with myself and script editor Peter Vincent making final edits and additions to this week's crop of news items. From an average of one hundred and fifty news items submitted six days before, we have whittled the list down to our final eighteen and we are still crossing the t's and dotting the i's. The news section lasts about four and a half minutes, but in terms of research, phone-calls, re-writes and general agonising, must take up more of our time than the remaining forty minutes of the show. The reward, however, is the sound of laughter that greets one of the classics, such as the Elephant Joke mentioned by Ronnie Barker. And we hope *you* are able to recapture the atmosphere of the Two Ronnies by reading this assortment from the last five years of the series.

TERRY HUGHES 1977
Producer of *The Two Ronnies*.

In a packed show tonight . . .

Ronnie Corbett: Good evening. It's nice to be with you again, isn't it Ronnie?

Ronnie Barker: Yes it is and in a packed show tonight we'll be talking by long distance phone to a Scotsman who found an Australian penny and emigrated.

RC: Then we'll talk to a stereo expert about his favourite breakfast –
two bowls of rice crispies ten feet apart.

RB: And we'll talk to the Texas man who made a fortune selling smokeless fuel to Red Indian couples who are not speaking to each other.

RC: And to a famous one fingered pickpocket who only steals Polo mints.

RB: And then a lady who's a world authority on carpets, an expert on rugs, and not at all bad on lino.

RC: And a hokey cokey champion who's just been disqualified for putting it in when he should have been shaking it all about.

RB: Next we'll interview three French film directors, Jacques Tati, Jacques Scruffi and Jacques Absolutely Falling to Pieces . . .

RC: Then the Romford girl who took the pill washed down with pond water and was today diagnosed as three months stagnant.

RB: Then we'll talk to two inventors, a gunsmith who's invented a sage and onion bullet so you can shoot the goose and stuff it at the same time -

RC: And the insecticide maker who's just produced an aphrodisiac for flies. It doesn't kill them but it lets you swat them two at a time.

RB: Then we'll interview the groundsman who used pansy seed instead of grass seed and queered his pitch.

RC: And a fifty-year-old doctor who claims that smoking takes years off your life. He says that if he hadn't smoked when he was younger he'd now be 63.

RB: Then we'll be talking to Mr. Herbert Gudge who has tattooed the whole of his body with old masters. He has a Botticelli on his chest, a Constable under each arm, a Watteau down the back, a Whistler up the front - (and the inscrutable smile of the Mona Lisa becomes a broad grin whenever he sits down . . .

*   *   *

RC: And now a sketch about two
workers in a ball bearing
factory, in which I play a
man who loses his bearings -

RB: And I play a man who loses
his temper.

*   *   *

crazy crossings . . .

Ronnie Corbett: Tonight we talk to a remarkable man who crossed a Rhode Island Red with a waitress and got a chicken that lays tables.

Ronnie Barker: Then he crossed a truss with a polo mint and got a Nutcracker Suite.

RC: - And a morse code transmitter with a sennapod and got dot dot dot and a very quick dash.

RB: He even crossed a food mixer with a nymphomaniac with a lisp - and got a girl who'll whisk anything.

RC: And a feather with a lady contortionist and got a girl who could tickle her own fancy.

RB: And he actually crossed a table tennis ball with an extremely tall chamber pot and got a ping pong piddle-high poe.

RC: Then we'll talk to a breeder who crossed a dog with a hen and got a poodle that cocks its own doodle.

RB: And a showbiz chef who crossed Raquel Welch with a packet of Bisto and got gravy with very big lumps.

RC: And a chemist who crossed a budgie with a laxative and got a chirrup of figs.

RB: And an Oxford butcher who crossed a turkey with an octopus so the boat crew could have a leg each.

RC: And an expert in animal husbandry who crossed a hen with a banjo and got a chicken that plucks itself.

RB: And a sporting man who crossed a tin of baked beans with two cricket bats and got wind in the willows.

RC: And a scientist who crossed a lady's hairpiece with a tomcat and a duck and got a plait billed duckypus.

RB: And a lady scientist who crossed the theories of Sigmund Freud with those of Albert Einstein and got sex at the speed of light.

RC: And an interior decorator who crossed an elephant with an Axminster rug and got a thick pile on his carpet.

RB: And a very *very* unlucky man. He crossed an enormous pear tree with a couple of blue tits . . . and got an enormous pair of blue trees . . .

RC: And we've just heard sensational news from Whipsnade. The male panda, who's developed a passion for music, has mated with the Head Keeper's harmonium. Experts say this may create a pandamonium.

*   *   *

RB: In the sketch that follows, I shall be practising for the Eisteddfod.

RC: And I shall be practising for the Lowsteddfod.

*   *   *

but later on tonight . . .

Ronnie Barker: Later on tonight we discuss the burning question about pilfering coalminers - do they have lots of slack in their trousers?

Ronnie Corbett:	And for the ladies we'll be talking about rum baba's - and what to wear if you've got them.
RB:	Then we'll be discussing potholing and why it ruins your bedroom carpets.
RC:	And a very wealthy man who was a snow-plough driver in Trinidad will tell us how he fiddled his overtime.
RB:	And in our new series *Medical Hints by Well Known Actresses* tonight your very own Googie Withers - and what to do if it does.
RC:	Later a well known patriotic gambler will tell us why he's backing Britain - he's getting two thousand to one against.

RB: And we'll find out what it's like to act as a stand-in for Raquel Welch –
in a special interview with Yul Brynner and Telly Savalas.

RC: And we'll have a feature on weeny boppers –
and how you shouldn't make fun of people who've got them.

RB: Then we'll interview a man whose parents were a clairvoyant and a contortionist and as a result he can foresee his own end.

RC: After that a Scottish vicar will be telling all children to say their prayers at night –
because you can send cheap rate messages after six o'clock.

RB: Lastly we'll be interviewing a very sexy interior decorator and his wife who fall out of bed every night because they prefer a matt finish . . .

at this point we were to have
said . . .

Ronnie Corbett: We were to have had Jimmy Saville with us but we've just heard that his suit has been disallowed by the Noise Abatement Society.

Ronnie Barker: And we're sorry to say that after further objections about West Indian bouncers, we've cancelled tonight's demonstration by the Trinidad Ladies Go-Go Dancers.

tonight's music . . .

Ronnie Corbett: Tonight we'll hear an excerpt from the new Grand Opera, *Eskimo Nell* — in which a seventeen stone contralto sings *You're Tiny . . . And it's Frozen . . .*

* * *

RB: In the sketch that follows, about Teddy boys and topless girls at a dance, I knock around with a pair of rockers -

RC: And I rock around with a pair of . . . Notts County footballers.

* * *

but first, the news . . .

Ronnie Barker:	But first, here is the news. The pound had another good day yesterday. It rose sharply at ten o'clock then had a light breakfast and went for a stroll in the park.
Ronnie Corbett:	This contrasts with last week when the pound closed at only 2.4 against the Matabele Gumbo Bead.
RB:	And shares fell 36 points when the Bank of England announced a closing down sale.
RC:	However, in a white paper today the Government revealed plans for the small shopkeeper - a lower counter.
RB:	And the Chancellor has announced new plans for shortening the dole queues. He's asking the men to stand closer together.

RC: And the Prime Minister announced today a new plan to ensure that we don't all suddenly become poor when we reach sixty - he's going to make sure we're all poor when we reach thirty.

RB: The Prime Minister went on to say that the state of the economy was in no way connected with the arrest this morning on Dover Beach of a large group of illegal immigrants who were trying to leave the country.

RC: Later, at Downing Street, the Premier was met by a delegation of squatters - but they wouldn't let him in.

RB: There was an embarrassing incident at Madame Tussaud's last week when Mr. Denis Healey unveiled the wax model of himself and his chauffeur drove it back to Westminster by mistake. Luckily it had only attended three cabinet meetings before it was discovered.

RC: And a secret diary just published reveals what MPs ate for their Christmas dinners last year. It seems Mr. Callaghan had the usual turkey -
while Mrs. Thatcher bought a new one.

RB: After an all-night sitting in the House of Commons all parties have now agreed it must have been the curry.

RC: In one dramatic incident last night, Mr. Cyril Smith rose from the Liberal Front Bench - and the rest of the party fell off the other end.

RB: At the end of a heated session tempers cooled in the Commons bar. Mr. Callaghan bought Mrs. Thatcher a pink gin, she bought Mr. Powell a black gin and he bought Mr. Wedgwood-Benn a pint of evostik.

RC: Foreign news. Uganda. At the state dinner to welcome the German delegation today, General Amin ate a hamburger, two frankfurters and a young man from Heidelburg.

RB: And news has just come in from Magalumbu, the primitive Pacific island where a man has been condemned to death for cannibalism. This morning, the day of the execution, the condemned man rose, got dressed, cleaned his teeth and ate a hearty warder.

                                    *   *   *

RB: But now a sketch set in
                Frankenstein's castle in
                which I take the very
                important part of the
                monster.

RC: And I make him put it back.

                                    *   *   *

royalty . . .

Ronnie Barker: Following the dispute with
the Domestic Servants Union
at Buckingham Palace today,
The Queen, a radiant figure
in white silk gown and
crimson robe, swept down the
main staircase and through
the hall — then she dusted the
cloakroom and hoovered the loun

Ronnie Corbett: And in the show jumping at
the Badminton Horse Trials,
Princess Anne once again left
her mark.
So he had to go home by bus.

* * *

RB: And we have just heard that
a man who broke into the
Royal Palace at Monaco and
tried to escape wearing shoes
belonging to Prince Rainier's
son and a dress belonging to
his wife — has been charged
with putting on heir's and
Grace's.

* * *

news from industry . . .

Ronnie Barker: Figures released today show that two out of every ten men work for a nationalised industry. While the other eight sit and watch them.

Ronnie Corbett: But a retiring Liverpool docker aged 65 stated that he'd never had a day's illness in his life - he always made it last a week.

RB: And Sir Hartley Chintz, the famous upholstery expert who yesterday fell into a fabric loom, is said to be almost completely recovered.

RC: And we've just heard that despite the strike of car delivery drivers at British Leyland, the 1000th car rolled off the assembly lines at four o'clock today - and fell onto a heap of 999 other cars. And that other strikers have been fitting silencers to the motor horns - and now the cars don't give a hoot either.

RB: But better news from the National Coal Board. they say there was no absenteeism in British pits last month. All the absentees stayed at home.

RC: At the Do-It-Yourself furniture competition at Olympia the favourite was Mrs. Cynthia Bollinger with her mahogany desk. But we've now heard she was disqualified at the last minute. Her legs were too bowed and when the Judge banged her bottom her drawers fell off.

RB: The President of the Winetasters' Association today paid tribute to their retiring secretary, Mrs. Prudence Vine. He described her as 'plucky and full bodied and well worth laying down for a couple of years'.

RC: Business mergers. We've just heard that Achilles Cleaning Powder have joined up with Scottish Distilleries to produce a cleaner that kills 99% of all known germs – and makes the other 1% too drunk to bother.

RB: And Mothercare are joining British Leyland to produce a car with a built-in rattle.

* * *

RC: In the sketch that follows, I'll be playing a man whose wife left him for the dustman.

RB: And I'll be playing the dustman who refuses to take him.

* * *

meet the workers . . .

Ronnie Corbett:	Later, in our series, *Meet the Workers,* we'll talk to an East End docker who has retired after forty years to take a well-earned job.
Ronnie Barker:	Then we'll interview the lady family planning officer who had triplets this week-end and was sacked for failing to report an accident.
RC:	Here's a piece of late news. Mr. Arthur Perkiss, the man who this week won £500,000 on the pools, has announced that he will never work another day in his life. So he's staying on with British Rail.

*   *   *

RB:	In the sketch that follows, *The Public and Private Lives of Samuel Pepys* — I play the public parts.
RC:	And I play the piano.

*   *   *

the rewards of industry . . .

Ronnie Corbett: Mr. Nigel Whipster, a window dresser for thirty years, today received the Queen's Award for Industry - and his flat mate, Rupert, received the Industry's Award for Queens.

Ronnie Barker: The man who invented the zip fastener was today honoured with a life peerage. He'll now be know as the Lord of the Flies.

RC: Tremendous results have been achieved by a team of British scientists who made ten laboratory rats smoke twenty cigarettes a day for a whole year. For this the team has been awarded the Nobel Prize - and the rats have got a colour telly with the coupons.

RB: The annual London *Health and Beauty* contest was won today by Miss Wapping. Second was Miss Not-Quite-So-Wapping, and third was Miss Absolutely-Piffling.

RC: Agriculture. Mr. Ernest Waldron, a cattle expert who's spent his whole life examining the back legs of cows, was given a special award today. Said Mr. Waldron, 'This is not the first time I've had a pat on the back.'

RB: The title of most considerate father of the year goes to Mr. Clarence Larkin of Stroud. He put a silencer on his shot gun because his daughter wanted a quiet wedding.

the world of medicine . . .

Ronnie Corbett:	The National Health Service state today they're getting so behindhand that for the Pregnancy Testing Service there is now a ten month waiting list.
Ronnie Barker:	But at Golders Green Maternity Hospital the wife of a well known ventriloquist has just given birth to a nine pound gouncing gagy goy.
RC:	And a spokesman from Warbleton Cottage Hospital said today there was no need to operate on the man who swallowed half a scrabble set. He said the problem will eventually solve itself though not in so many words.

RB: In a new drive to improve the standards of service and hygiene a West End Hotel today dismissed a waiter for having his thumb in the soup . . . They also dismissed a topless waitress for two similar offences.

RC: A young woman from
          Wealdstone made an
          extremely serious complaint
          today against a famous
          cosmetic surgeon. She said he
          gave her a perfect bust but
          made it far too big. Having
          weighed the evidence, the
          Police have put it in the
          hands of the Public
          Prosecutor.

RB: And we've just heard that
          National Health doctors have
          staged a protest march down
          Harley Street waving big
          placards written out by
          themselves. Unfortunately no
          one could read the placards
          except one chemist who was
          passing. He told them to
          come back in ten minutes.

RC: In another complaint against the Health Service a patient said he was rushed around the country for a series of emergency operations. He had a hand operation at Neasden and a knee operation at Handsworth. Then he had a heart transplant at Liverpool and a liver transplant at Hartlepool.

RB: - Then he had a hair transplant at Littlehampton and on arriving at Harefield he fainted.

*   *   *

RC: But now a sketch about ghosts and ghouls in which I get caught by the ghosties -

RB: - And I get caught by surprise.

*   *   *

we apologise for the late
arrival of . . .

Ronnie Corbett: British Rail announce that they have developed a new engine so fast that it can travel from London to Reading before its driver gets a pay rise.

Ronnie Barker: And British Rail research scientists have come up with a new serum for the common cold. It doesn't cure the cold but your nose will only run in good weather.

RC: There was chaos at King's
        Cross today when a
        consignment of 93 tortoises
        from Indonesia escaped from
        a guard's van and made off
        along the platform. When
        asked how the tortoises
        managed to get clean away
        the Stationmaster said, 'We
        tried to stop them but they
        were just too fast for our
        porters.'

RB: And some happy news from British Rail. Agatha Wainwright, the station announcer at Victoria, today married engine driver Dick Crankshawe. Her dress was of white organdie with lace bodice and her train was twenty minutes late.

RC: Other good news: British Rail won their case against a party of Rabbis today. They claimed that though they were indeed the Children of Israel, this didn't entitle them to travel half fare.

showbiz . . .

Ronnie Barker: Shirley Bassey has just had a single come out . . . one of the straps broke on her dress.

Ronnie Corbett: And due to heavy fog in Central London, Susan Hampshire, who's playing Peter Pan, couldn't land at the Colosseum and had to be diverted to Manchester Opera House.

RB: From Hollywood Zsa Zsa Gabor has announced that owing to illness she has cancelled all her engagements for three months - but her marriages will go ahead as planned.

RC: And there's good news for
       deaf people.
       The Rolling Stones issued
       another LP today.

sports news . . .

Ronnie Corbett: In the International Relay event at the White City today, the Irish 4 by 400 metres team built up a commanding lead before handing the baton to the Russian team.

Ronnie Barker: Whilst in the nudists' pentathlon at the Hendon Naturedrome, Britain's Orville Stark was fourth in the hundred metres, third in the long jump, second in the low hurdles, had an accident in the high hurdles - and easily won the yodelling.

RC: And there's news from Japan that Mr. Watanabe Akimoto, the winner of the slow bicycle race in the 1972 Olympics, has just completed his lap of honour.

RB: And Mr. Ernest Quigley, the winner of the sponsored hairdressing marathon who's had his hair permed and set non-stop for 73 hours, was today described as completely and utterly lacquered.

RC: And in an exclusive interview last night, Britain's best known show jumping husband, Captain Philip Dugdale, told our reporter that his first year of marriage had been almost perfect. His bride, Anthea Ascot-Jones, had only six faults, he said, and two of those were refusals. Next year he was hoping for a clear round.

RC: Reports that athletes indulge in too much sex before meetings were hotly denied by sprinter Wellesley Blunt. He went on to win the hundred metres in a time of two hours thirty seven minutes.

START

RB:　　　　　　　Finally, it's been revealed in
a report laid before the
International Olympic
Committee that at the last
Olympic Games several
athletes took steroids, the
Russian gymnast Anna
Volga took annaroids,
Anthony Armstrong-Jones
took several polaroids and
David Hemery took syrup of
figs.

and now the weather . . .

Ronnie Corbett: Here's tomorrow's weather forecast: the sun will be killing 'em in Gillingham, it'll be choking in Woking, dry in Rye and cool in Goole. And if you live in Lissingdown take an umbrella.

stop press!

Ronnie Barker: A survey on the decline of morals in Britain reveals that in Liverpool alone on each day last week an average of 267 women made love to an unmarried man.
The man is now recovering in hospital.

Ronnie Corbett: Mr. Osbert Grove, Britain's worst ever postman, who claims he was wrongfully dismissed by the GPO, today delivered a petition to the Queen — at 15 Station Street, Scunthorpe.

RB: News from the Church. After weeks of speculation, death watch beetle has been confirmed in Canterbury Cathedral.
The Archbishop also confirmed three mice, two bats and a spider.

RC: While Catholic missionaries in Matabeleland are reporting progress with a tribe of cannibals. They're not completely cured but they are improving. On Fridays they only eat fishermen.

RB: News from the Irish. There was a disturbance at Hampton Court Maze this afternoon. A party of Irish trippers panicked when they couldn't find their way in.

RC: And it was announced today in Dublin that the Irish Doomsday Book is in fact a forgery. This was the conclusion after a six month study of it by typewriting experts.

RB: From the world of nature in the raw comes first the news that a female streaker disturbed patrons at the Albert Hall today. Luckily she was caught by the bouncers and ejected.

RC: And a Watford man has made a serious complaint against the Sunnyview Naturists' Paradise. He said that after being in the nudist camp for at least three months he had a letter from the secretary that began, 'Dear Sir or Madam . . .'

RB: Another disappointed guest at Sunnyview was a member of the Charles Dickens Society's annual nudist weekend. He had Great Expectations but it was a very Bleak House and everybody laughed at his Little Dorritt.

RC: The funeral took place today of Mr. Spencer P. Dobson, the famous compiler of crossword puzzles. After a short service he was buried six down and three across.

RB: And we've just heard that the West Drayton man who kept himself awake every night for seventeen years by snoring, has at last found the answer. He's going to sleep in another room.

RC: Finally there's a report today from the team who've been investigating the social habits of Mr. and Mrs. Average. Unfortunately Mr. Average was not at home. He'd slipped down to Brighton with Mrs. Well-Above-Average.

now here are the notices ...

Ronnie Barker: There'll be a conference and sermon in the Free Church Hall tomorrow for those who thirst after righteousness. — And for those who thirst *before* righteousness, the *Cat and Fiddle* opens early.

Ronnie Corbett: Meanwhile the Ministry of Agriculture have advice for all of you who are troubled by flies in your kitchen . . . put a load of manure in your living room.

RB: And British Rail announce a new service for naughty couples going to Brighton — the have-it-away-day.

RC: McCleod's Cinema in Peebles opens today with a special offer. Old age pensioners are admitted free — if accompanied by their parents.

RB: The powerful secret society known as *The Lords of the Universe* would have held their annual meeting last night. But their President, the Lord Chief Controller and Commander Over All Living Things, was unable to be present. His wife wouldn't let him out.

RC: And we end with an important message from the Royal Society for the Prevention of Accidents. Since most accidents happen in your home — they advise you to move.

but now a sketch . . .

Ronnie Corbett: But now a sketch featuring Mr. Ronnie Barker who only today was presented with an illuminated address by his neighbours — they set his house on fire.

Ronnie Barker: And now a sketch featuring Mr. Ronnie Corbett who this year made a lot of money on the greyhounds — as a jockey.

RC: And featuring Mr. Ronnie Barker, a man who's so modest that when he recently published his autobiography he wasn't even mentioned in it.

RB: And Mr. Ronnie Corbett who in fact buys all his suits off the peg —
at any shop selling Action Man.

RC: And now a sketch in which Mr. Ronnie Barker plays the part of a bridegroom who finds there is no bed in the honeymoon suite and has to stand up for his conjugal rights.

RB: In the sketch that follows, Ronnie Corbett was to have starred in his own version of *Jaws*, but unfortunately the goldfish died.

but now here's the late news
— disasters and accidents . . .

Ronnie Corbett: Reports are coming in that an elephant has done the ton on the M1. Motorists are advised to use great caution and treat it as a roundabout.

Ronnie Barker: And another motoring flash. On the A30 this afternoon a tanker-load of bleach on its way to the West Country overturned on a notorious accident black spot, turning it immediately into a notorious accident white spot.

RB: And there was an accident involving Britain's worst goalkeeper, Bill Berkley, who has already let through 157 goals this season. Shouting out 'I am a complete failure, ' Berkley threw himself in front of a bus ... luckily the bus passed under him and he wasn't hurt.

RB: At a factory in Walsall today
the prototype of a mammoth
50 foot high food mixer went
completely out of control.
The entire company has gone
into liquidation.

but we've just heard . . .

Ronnie Barker: We've just heard that the three desperate criminals who escaped from Dartmoor yesterday in appalling weather conditions, have been recaptured.
One was in Jersey, another in Cardigan and the third was in a nice woolly jumper his mummy made.

Ronnie Corbett: And we've just heard that a cement mixer has collided with a prison van on the Kingston By-Pass. Motorists are asked to be on the look out for 16 hardened criminals.

B: And in the English Channel a ship carrying red paint has collided with a ship carrying purple paint. It is believed that both crews have been marooned.

C: Sir Hartley Fawcett, crackshot big game hunter, famous for his slogan, 'Shoot 'm right between the eyes!' — was eaten late last night by two one-eyed tigers walking arm in arm.

RB: And we've just heard that Mr. Arnold Limpkin, the famous one-legged tap dancer, retired today. A special programme tonight features some of his greatest hits, like *I Could Have Hopped All Night, Knee up Mother Brown* and *Twenty Tiny Fingers Fifteen Tiny Toes.*

crime . . .

Ronnie Barker: Following an incident in Oxford Street involving three lady shoppers and a policeman's truncheon, Mr. Bert Whizzer, a one-man band, has been charged with conducting himself improperly.

Ronnie Corbett: 8000 cases of imported fruit were stolen from Liverpool docks today. A police spokesman said, 'It would have taken a gang of dock thieves at least four hours to do this.' A spokesman for the dockers said, 'What happens in the tea break is none of our concern.'

RB: A pickpocket who was chased
out of Battersea Funfair took
refuge today in the Post
Office Tower. Police
immediately threw a ring
round it — and the
Postmaster General gave
them a goldfish.

RC: 'Police are clamping down on
dealers who make fortunes
selling stolen cars which have
been sawn in half and welded
to other vehicles,' — said
Superintendent Hackett from
the wheel of his E type
combine harvester today.

RB: A man who threw his mother-in-law into the crocodile pool at Belleview Zoo has been prosecuted by the RSPCA.

RC:
In another incident, West Kensington police questioned a man with a wooden leg who was hopping down the High Street while pouring a tin of treacle over his bald head. The man explained that he was going to a fancy dress ball as a toffee apple.

RC: Arnold Higgins, a council architect from Cheshire, was today charged with seducing his secretary on his own drawing board and consigning two thousand people to live in a huge pair of panties in Runcorn.

RB: And a man was detained at Saville Row Police Station today after an incident involving a topless model in an Oxford Street store window. He was later arrested and charged with a smash and two grabs.

RC: Mr. George Thrakes, the building contractor who was gaoled last year for supplying millions of poundsworth of defective building materials to the Government, escaped from Wormwood Scrubs today when the front fell off.

and offences against
decency . . .

Ronnie Barker: Complaints were made following the Chef's Annual Fancy Dress Ball last night. It seems a woman dressed only in gooseberries and cream made improper suggestions to a man dressed in cake and sherry. She made a proper fool of herself and got a trifle excited.

Ronnie Corbett: Mr. Patrick O'Flynn of Dublin was arrested today for streaking through a nudist camp.

RB: And a woman who paraded through the streets of Pontefract yesterday, naked except for a contact lens on each bosom, has been arrested for making a spectacle of herself.

RC: Streakers in the Greater London area are now being faced with Scotland Yard's latest counter-measure; police dogs with wet noses.

RB: But it seems the perfect crime was committed last night when thieves broke into Scotland Yard itself and stole all the toilets. Police say they haven't a single thing to go on.

and news from the courts . . .

Ronnie Barker:	The longest ever swearing-in of a witness ended in the High Court this afternoon after 6½ days when the witness, Bert Osby, instead of holding the Bible and reading out the card, held the card and read out the Bible.
Ronnie Corbett:	Lord Chief Justice Harris today laid down the maximum penalty for bigamy: two mothers-in-law.

RB: A mother of three today filed a paternity suit against a cricketer who fielded in the deep. Asked on what grounds she replied, 'Trent Bridge, The Oval and behind the sight screen at Battersea Park.'

RC: And a man who broke into Brigitte Bardot's bedroom and laid his hands on her jewellery has been found guilty but insane.

RB: The world's most stupid man, Mr. Brodrik Godbolt, was today found not guilty of trying to gas his wife by throwing her into the North Sea.

RC: A vicar who rode his bicycle the wrong way up the M6 was asked in court how on earth he managed to avoid an accident. He replied, 'God was with me'. He was further charged with riding two on a bike.

RB: And in a very serious case in the High Court this afternoon an eighteen-year-old secretary in the Foreign Office confessed that she disgraced herself at an Embassy Reception by entertaining a Russian spy on the bedroom carpet, the Mayor of Helsinki in the garbage can, a Chinese attache in the washbasin, a Prussian officer in the fuel receptacle and an African Chief in the downstairs toilet. Summing up, the Judge said she had a Red under the bed, a Finn in the bin, a Chink in the sink, a Junker in the bunker and a Swazi in the khasi . . .

in the central divorce court today . . .

Ronnie Corbett: In the Central Divorce Court today a man told the Judge that his wife, an enthusiastic traffic warden, had painted double yellow lines round her waist — and had booked him fifteen times already this month.

Ronnie Barker: He didn't mind paying the fines but he did object when she kept towing him away.

RC: And a woman from Warrington gained a divorce on the grounds that whenever lightning flashed in the night her husband jumped up shouting 'I'll buy the negatives.'

RB: Another lady, a clairvoyant from Carshalton, was granted a divorce on the grounds of her husband's adultery next weekend in Brighton.

RC: And an 85-year-old farmer divorced his seventeen-year-old wife because he couldn't keep his hands off her. He's now sacked his hands and bought a combine harvester.

RB: The divorce was announced today of John Rupert Prendegast and William Henry Smithers. Breakdown of the marriage was due to incompatibility and a short sighted vicar.

RC: In the last case a traffic light manufacturer was granted a divorce on the grounds that his wife only ever wore three nightdresses; a red one which meant 'Stop — you can't go.' — a flashing yellow one which meant, 'You may go but give way to pedestrians,' and a red and amber one which meant, 'You may go only if you have started or are so close to the line that to stop suddenly might cause an accident.'

and a few items of late late
news . . .

Ronnie Corbett: We've just this moment heard that the two pandas at London Zoo have begun to mate. The winner meets Bobby Fischer in the final.

Ronnie Barker: And a Hull man has been prosecuted for cruelty by the RSPCA. He bought a homing pigeon and moved house.

RC: And it appears that in Hexham this evening a mad dog bit an income tax inspector. After being given injections and treatment for shock the dog has been allowed to go home.

RB: Meanwhile British Rail announce that the price of coffee is to go up to 15p a slice.

RC: And we've found out why Shepherds Bush town hall are flying the Royal standard at half mast — they're half expecting the Queen.

RB: And more news of the plumber from Didsbury who earlier today swallowed an immersion heater and a ballcock. He is now said to be comfortable apart from occasional hot flushes.

RC: The Ministry of Education have revealed some very interesting figures today. It seems that in the Birmingham area one half of the population can't read, one half can't write and the other three quarters can't add up.

RB: It's announced in Newport Pagnell this evening that Mr. Horace Whipsley, the world's most superstitious motorist, known for the lucky horseshoe dangling in his rear window, the sprig of heather on his wipers, the St. Christopher suspended from his dashboard and the four rabbit's feet in his glove compartment — was run over by thirteen steamrollers.

RC: And a last round-up from the courts. Thirty drunken trippers who nipped off their coach for a certain reason on Hammersmith Bridge just as the Cambridge crew were passing underneath have each been fined ten pounds for having one over the eight.

RB: And after a marriage lasting
only seven days a newspaper
editor's wife has filed a
petition for divorce on the
grounds that he is too small
a type, she's become bored
with his special features and
he refuses to give her a late
night extra.

RC: Here are two final items of
news. At the Royal Air Show
today, Luigi Bregnozi, the
famous drunken Italian air
ace, was not permitted to do
his celebrated dive through
the sound barrier. The
controller said he could not
endanger the crowd with a
high tiddley iteye boom
boom!

RB: And we've just been told the police are desperately seeking the man who steals the ends of news items. The man is described as tall and grey haired with a very big

well, that's all for this week . . .

Ronnie Corbett: Well, that's all for this week. Next week I'll be reviewing a book that's just become a best seller in Scotland, entitled *Indoor Games for Flag Days*.

Ronnie Barker: Then we'll have hints on coarse fishing ... followed by lewd hockey, suggestive cricket and obscene golf.

RC: Then we'll be demonstrating the very latest brassiere. It's called *The Sheepdog* — it rounds them up and points them in the right direction.

RB: Then we'll discuss the bread shortage with a man who's been throwing IOUs to the ducks.

RC: Then we'll look at some unusual dances including the Gay Gordons, the Nice Nigels and the Queer Quistophers.

RB: We'll be encouraging newlyweds to purchase their own building sites with the new government slogan 'Get lots while you're young'.

RC: And a famous millionaire will reveal how it feels to have piles of gold . . . wealthy but uncomfortable.

RB: We'll continue our investigation into the political beliefs of nudists. We've already noticed a definite swing to the left —

RC: And we'll have with us a man who is so superstitious he got stuck in a lift with thirteen strippers and pressed the alarm button.

RB: And a Sultan with 365 wives
              will explain to us why he's
              looking forward to leap year.

RC: Then there'll be music. We'll
              hear the oldest bagpiper in
              Scotland, Mr. Jock
              McDougal, who in World
              War One played so well in
              battle that the enemy used to
              shout out requests.

RB: Then we'll have three contrasting pieces of choral music; sacred songs from St. Martin-in-the-Fields, rather less sacred songs from St. Christopher-in-the-Woods and some positively revolting songs from St. Vitus-in-the-Long-Grass-Behind-the-Glue-Factory.

RC: And we'll even hear the band of the Royal Cross-eyed Dragoons who'll play *The Dance of the Sugar Plum Sailor* followed by *What Shall we do With the Drunken Fairy?*

RB: Meanwhile we'll be running a competition in Blackpool. Eddie Waring will be buried in the sand and the first kiddie to dig him up will get a thick ear.

RC: Then it's novelty time. Miss Rita Metricata who dresses only in three coins will do a dance. We're letting her come on as she's down to her last penny.

RB: After this, Antonio, the famous Spanish dancer, will be showing us how to dance the fandango — with his fan in one hand and his dango in the other.

RC: As a finale a very lovely young physical education mistress will do a novelty dance covered only in blackboard chalk — but the novelty soon wears off.

RB: We'll end with two rather unusual items. We'll have with us Mr. Dudley Wilford who yesterday on his hundredth birthday was arrested for chasing 23 young women at an athletics meeting. He received a summons from the court and a telegram of congratulation from the Queen.

RC: Then we'll see Fanny Craddock starring in her new play, *Lady Windermere's Flan;* a lady who used to grow grass on her chest will present *How Green Was my Valley.* And a man who lives next to a sewage works will read from his journal, *The House at Poo Corner.*

RB: We'll end by discussing a burning question that many of you have asked. 'What should you tip the porter in all-male nudist camp — and will a pound note cover it?'

*   *   *

RC:	Well, that's all we've got room for in this book — isn't it Ronnie?
RB:	Yes it is and that means it's —
RC:	Goodnight from me —
RB:	And it's goodnight from him.
BOTH:	Goodnight!

*   *   *

HUMOUR

0352		Star	
		Woody Allen	
	300698	**GETTING EVEN**	**50p***
		Alida Baxter	
	398973	**FLAT ON MY BACK**	**50p**
	397101	**UP TO MY NECK**	**50p**
		Alex Duncan	
	397020	**VETS IN THE BELFRY**	**50p**
	398612	**IT'S A VET'S LIFE**	**60p**
	398795	**THE VET HAS NINE LIVES**	**50p**
		Stephen John	
	397535	**WHAT A WAY TO GO!**	**50p**
		Jack Millmay	
	397527	**REVELATIONS FROM THE RAG TRADE**	**50p**
		Stanley Morgan	
	398965	**RUSS TOBIN'S BEDSIDE GUIDE TO SMOOTHER SEDUCTION**	**60p**

*Not for sale in Canada

HUMOUR

0426		Tandem	
	158350	Tony Blackburn **A LAUGH IN EVERY POCKET**	40p
	075870	Hugh Burnett **'Those Marvellous Monks!'** (cartoons) **BEWARE OF THE ABBOT**	25p
	075951	**BOOK OF THE MONK**	25p
	07579X	**NOTHING SACRED**	25p
	075609	**SACRED & CONFIDENTIAL**	25p
	076087	**TOP SACRED**	25p
	136616	**DARLING — YOU ARE A DEVIL!**	50p*
	076249	Lynda Mallet **ALL BRA YESTERDAYS**	50p*
	07632X	**MALLET'S BRA BOOK**	50p*
	139607	Spike Milligan **THE BEDSIDE MILLIGAN**	30p
	139879	**A BOOK OF BITS OR A BIT OF A BOOK**	30p
	139526	**A DUSTBIN OF MILLIGAN**	30p
	139798	**THE LITTLE POT BOILER**	30p
	165470	**SEXY CROSSWORDS**	50p*
	157559	Hugh de Witt **BAWDY BARRACK-ROOM BALLADS**	35p

*Not for sale in Canada

Wyndham Books are obtainable from many booksellers and newsagents. If you have any difficulty please send purchase price plus postage on the scale below to:

**Wyndham Cash Sales
44 Hill Street
London W1X 8LB**

OR

**Star Book Service,
G.P.O. Box 29,
Douglas,
Isle of Man,
British Isles**

While every effort is made to keep prices low, it is sometimes necessary to increase prices at short notice. Wyndham Books reserve the right to show new retail prices on covers which may differ from those advertised in the text or elsewhere.

Postage and Packing Rate

U.K. & Eire
One book 15p plus 7p per copy for each additional book ordered to a maximum charge of 57p.

These charges are subject to Post Office charge fluctuations.